THE LITTLE BOOK OF
CURRY TIPS

AN

G000058587

THE LITTLE BOOK OF CURRY TIPS

ANDREW LANGLEY

Absolute Press

First published in Great Britain in 2010 by
Absolute Press
Scarborough House, 29 James Street West
Bath BA1 2BT, England
Phone 44 (0) 1225 316013 **Fax** 44 (0) 1225 445836
E-mail info@absolutepress.co.uk
Web www.absolutepress.co.uk

Copyright 2010 © Andrew Langley

The rights of Andrew Langley to be identified as the author of this work have been asserted by him in accordance with the Copyright Designs and Patents Act 1988.

All rights reserved. No part of this publication may be reproduced, stored in a retrieval system or transmitted in any form or by any means, electronic or otherwise, without the prior permission of Absolute Press.

A catalogue record of this book is available from the British Library

ISBN 13: 9781906650247

Printed and bound in Malta on behalf of Latitude Press

‘This curry was like a performance of
Beethoven’s Ninth Symphony...
especially the last movement, with
everything screaming and banging ‘Joy.’

Anthony Burgess (1917–1993),
English writer

1

Remember that curry is now part of global culture. The word is used in Europe and America to describe the kinds of spiced dishes which originated in southern Asia. Curry has travelled across the world, and most countries have adapted it to suit themselves. Nobody owns it.

2

Spicy food such as curry does help you cool down.

Spices themselves are not 'thermally' hot. They (and chilli in particular) make us feel hotter than we actually are, and stimulate our cooling responses, such as sweating. Spicy dishes also speed up our metabolic rate, causing us to burn up energy more quickly.

3

A curry, like a casserole, always tastes better next day

(or even the day after that). Cook it at least a day early if you possibly can, then cool it and keep it in the fridge overnight. This allows time for the spices to mingle and develop, and adds great breadth and subtlety to the overall flavour.

4

Basic curry ingredients #1: the spices.

These may vary according to taste or region. There is no officially-recognized mixture, though most curries have two core elements: cumin seed and coriander seed. Apart from these, important spices include fenugreek, turmeric, cardamom and black or red pepper.

5

Always use fresh spices or curry powder.

Any finely ground spice will lose its potency in a short time: the finer the grind, the faster the flavour molecules will escape. If you're buying ground spices, make sure you trust the supplier to be selling as fresh as possible, and use it up within a month.

6

The best way to ensure of freshness is to

grind your own whole spices as you need them.

You can use one of the new-fangled shakers, an electric coffee mill or the good old pestle and mortar. But the best machine is a hand coffee grinder (cleaned out), which can be turned more slowly.

7

Pre-chill your grinder and spices in the fridge.

This will make sure that they are as cool as possible before grinding. The action of crushing and grinding produces heat, and heat makes the aroma molecules escape more quickly. This is the best way of preserving the original character of each spice.

8

Make your own blend of garam masala,

one of the basic spice mixes for curry dishes. Gently heat 4 tablespoons of coriander seed, 1 tablespoon each of cumin seed and peppercorns, 4 cardamom pods, 10 cloves and half a cinnamon stick in a dry pan till the seeds pop (no more than 5 minutes). Cool, husk the cardamom and grind together.

9

Label your spice jars. Whole spices are easy enough to identify, but ground spices often look indistinguishable. Can you tell ground cumin from ground coriander, for example? When you empty a packet or bag of loose ground spice into a jar, put a label on straightaway. Write the name of the spice and the date you bought it.

10

Basic curry ingredients #2: the chilli. There are dozens of different varieties and potencies, from the ferocious *bhut jolokia* to the relatively friendly jalapeno or paprika. The most common chilli used in curries is the green cayenne pepper, but for a bigger blast try habaneros (or scotch bonnets).

11

Chilli Rules #1: always add chilli gradually to a dish.

Start off sparingly – you can always put in more later on if you wish. However, if you put in too much you can never take it out again. This approach is especially important if you're not quite sure how strong your chilli is.

12

Though nothing to do with curry spices,

the leaves of the curry tree

are widely used in the cookery of the subcontinent.

Buy them fresh

(dried leaves are greatly inferior) or grow them yourself. Sauté the crushed leaves in hot oil and add to dhals, vegetable dishes or coconut chutney.

13

Basic curry ingredients #3: the oil and fat.

All curries need fat in some form to soothe the spices and blend the flavours. Many Indian dishes call for ghee (clarified butter), which has a smooth and nutty flavour, but sunflower or groundnut oil can be used instead – and is the healthier option.

14

Making your own ghee is straightforward,

providing you watch it very closely. Melt unsalted organic butter in a pan over a medium/low heat. It will bubble up, then subside as the water evaporates. After about 20 minutes, the liquid turns amber. Remove from the heat immediately, and strain through muslin into an airtight jar.

15

Chilli Rules #2:

remember that **chillies tend to become less hot the longer they cook.** So if you want a milder curry, add the chilli earlier in the cooking. If, on the other hand, you want it hotter, add the chilli later (but not right at the end, or the flavours won't have a chance to take effect).

16

Basic curry ingredients #4: the body-builders.

The sauce needs 'body', but few curry dishes (especially Indian ones) use flour to achieve this. Instead, add finely chopped and sautéed onion and garlic, plus grated root ginger. For creaminess, you can put in yoghurt, coconut milk or ground almonds.

17

Toast or fry most whole spices

such as cumin, fennel seed, cardamom, black mustard and peppercorns. This is the first step in making most curries, and both releases and intensifies the flavours of the spices. Toast gently in a dry pan, or fry in oil or ghee (keep the oil, which will absorb the flavours).

18

The heart of almost any curry sauce is the humble onion – but treat it with respect.

Heat a generous slosh of oil over a medium heat in a frying pan, then add the finely chopped onion. Cook for at least 10 minutes, adjusting the heat to make sure it doesn't burn but turns translucent or golden.

19

Prepare a paste of ginger and garlic to follow the onion. Whizz up a knuckle-sized lump of peeled ginger root with 10–12 peeled garlic cloves in a blender. Mix in water to make a paste-like consistency. Add this to the hot oil in the pan once the onions are cooked. This is the base of most curry sauces.

20

Making your own poppadoms is easy

– with the right sort of flour. The best is urad lentil flour, but gram (chickpea) flour will do. Knead a cup of flour with a pinch of salt and enough water to make a thick paste. Season with pepper and cumin. Take about a spoon full, roll out very thin and deep fry in sunflower or groundnut oil.

21

Chicken *biryani* is a simple and speedy curry standby. In oil or ghee, brown cubed chicken breast and set aside. Then brown onions, spices (cardamom, cinnamon, bay) and some garlic and ginger paste and return the meat. After 10 minutes, add rice and water or stock. Cook gently for 25 minutes. Stir in toasted almonds.

22

Yoghurt has countless uses in curry-making.

It is a fine marinade, which tenderises potentially tough customers like goat or mutton. It thickens and creams sauces. And it forms the basis of many fine side dishes. Try mixing it with cucumber, cumin and mint, or with crushed roasted aubergine and a dash of cayenne.

23

Serve a tomato relish as a refresher alongside the heavier stuff.

Dice tomatoes with half the quantity of onion. Mix in with chopped parsley or coriander and dress with lemon juice, toasted cumin seed, a pinch of salt and just a touch of cayenne pepper.

24

Dhal is a soothing companion for spicy meat and vegetable dishes. The basis is a thick stew of pulses – usually red or green lentils, split peas, chick peas, black-eyed beans or mung beans. Cook with turmeric, ginger or asafoetida to make it more easily digestible.

25

Rogan josh
– the Kashmiri red mutton stew –
has conquered the world.

Fry mutton or goat cubes, then cardamom, bay, cloves and cinnamon, then the usual onions and ginger and garlic. Lastly, put in ground chilli (hence the redness). Return the meat, add a generous dollop of yoghurt and water to cover. Simmer for one hour.

26

Chilli Rules #3: know the strength of your chilli

– roughly. Red chillis tend to be at least twice as hot as green ones, and small red ones even hotter than that. Dried chillis are dramatically hotter (up to ten times) than fresh ones.

27

Wash and soak rice before you cook it.

Rinse (preferably basmati) rice in several changes of water, and stir it about with your fingers. This gets rid of much of the powdery starch. Then soak the rice in clean water for at least half-and-hour, to plump up the grains.

28

Gently sauté the rice before you add the water. Warm a little oil in the pan, add the well-drained rice and stir occasionally and delicately. The frying dries the raw rice and makes the grains less likely to stick together. After a minute or two, pour in water or stock to cover by an inch, and heat to simmering.

29

Treat your rice tenderly. Boiling too violently and lengthily is likely to turn it into what my granny called a 'clidge'. Simmer on the hob or in the oven at the lowest possible heat for 25 minutes, making sure the pan lid is tightly covered so that the steam stays inside (add some foil or a folded tea towel if necessary).

30

Spices add an extra dimension to basmati rice.

Sauté chopped onion in oil, then add well-soaked rice, plus garlic, garam masala and chopped green chilli. After a couple of minutes, pour in stock or water and cook carefully in the normal way. This spiced rice goes especially well with chicken or mutton dishes.

31

Pulao goes by many other names (pilaff, pilau, plov) throughout South Asia.

For a simple vegetable pulao, fry cumin seeds then onions and the ginger and garlic paste. Add chopped carrots, potatoes, peas and green beans. Stir in turmeric, coriander and chilli plus rice and then water and cook slowly for 25–30 minutes.

32

To make a (fairly) authentic Parsee dhansak, you need several key ingredients. One is lamb (rather than other meat). Others are agents to produce a sweet and sour flavour - the most obvious being sugar and lemon juice - as well as lentils. Among spices must be cumin, turmeric, cardamom – and plenty of chilli.

33

If you're in a hurry, by all means **use readymade curry powders** off the shelf. But remember two things. One: make sure they're as fresh as possible. And two: try mixing more than one brand of powder, as they will each have a slightly different combination of spices.

34

Chilli Rules #4: protect yourself when handling chillies.

Their oils will burn sensitive parts of the body, especially the eyes. Avoid handling them directly. When cutting them, wear gloves or use a fork with the knife. Wash the utensils separately.

35

You can make tandoori chicken without a tandoor.

Rub skinned chicken pieces with salt and lime juice, then marinade in a whizzed mixture of yoghurt, onion, garlic, ginger, paprika and garam masala for 24 hours. Pre-heat the oven to very hot and bake (or grill) the drained and oiled chicken pieces for about 20 minutes.

36

Paratha bread is a must with most curry dishes. Mix 450g (1lb) of mixed wholemeal and plain flour and a pinch of salt. Then rub in 2 tablespoons of ghee or oil and add enough tepid water to make into a soft dough. Knead and let rise. Divide into 10 or so balls, flatten them out, brush with oil and fold in two. Fry in more oil until golden.

37

Chicken dopiaza (double onions) is twice as oniony.

Sauté cumin seeds, then at least two large onions (chopped) until golden. Pop in some garam masala and garlic and ginger mix. Blend together with a tin of tomatoes, and use the result to poach chicken pieces for 20 minutes. Add more fried onion rings to serve.

38

Lamb and spinach make a magical combination in saag gosht.

Fry mustard seeds, then brown onions, lamb chunks and garlic and ginger mix. Add green chillies, turmeric, garam masala and plenty of chopped spinach. Finally stir in yoghurt and cook gently for one hour. Serve with rice or naan bread.

39

Vindaloo is about more than just chilli.

OK, so chilli is at the centre (the dried red variety), but you can adjust the amount to control the curry's potency. Also vital to the peculiar power of this dish is the host of other spices – cumin seed, peppercorns, black mustard seed, cinnamon, cardamom, fenugreek, coriander and turmeric.

40

Chilli Rules #5: drink milk to soothe that burning throat.

If you are finding things uncomfortably hot, have a glass of milk or – better still – a lassi. This is a Punjabi drink made by blending yoghurt, water, salt and ice, and flavoured with cumin or honey. Avoid water or lager at all costs.

41

Stop your rice from going clidgey.

Besides the rice-preparation advice already given here, the belt-and-braces approach is to add sugar and lemon juice to the grains after soaking and before cooking. This should prevent sticky lumpiness.

42

Give hard-boiled eggs the vindaloo treatment.

Fry a small piece of cinnamon stick, then add onions to soften. Stir in a mash of garlic, ginger, paprika, cumin, sugar and a little vinegar, plus some garam masala. After 2 minutes, dilute it with more vinegar, put in the halved eggs and cook gently for another 5 minutes.

43

Chicken korma uses another classic yoghurt marinade.

The mix is simple – yoghurt, garlic and ginger paste and ground coriander. Chill overnight. Unlike tandoori chicken, this cooks slowly with the marinade. Fry onions and green chillies, add meat and marinade and cook for 30 minutes. Stir in coconut and ground almonds.

44

Coriander relish is easy to make, and a fine accompaniment for curried meat. Simply whizz up a handful of fresh coriander, a green chilli, juice of half a lemon, toasted cumin seed, salt and pepper. Eat it quickly, as it won't last more than a day or two.

45

Learn to love lime pickle. Better still, pickle your own.

Cut 10 limes into wedges and pack in a glass jar. Add juice from 5 limes mixed with 2 tablespoons of salt, plus ground chilli, toasted mustard, cumin and fenugreek seeds. Seal and leave for two weeks. Lastly add mustard oil to cover. Start eating a week later.

46

Make your own chapatis.

Slowly add warm water to half a pint of *atta* (or fine-ground wholemeal) flour in a bowl, mixing it to a non-sticky dough. Knead and leave to prove for 40 minutes. Heat a good heavy skillet. Tear off balls of dough and roll them flat, then bake them in the skillet for no more than one minute per side.

47

Remember to add salt.

Spices add such a vast variety of flavours and taste sensations to a dish, that some cooks forget the salty part. Be judicious: taste the sauce towards the end of cooking and salt according to your judgement. If you put in too much, bung in a potato for 10 minutes to absorb the excess and then remove it

48

Chilli Rules #6: how to store fresh chillies.

Leave chilli peppers lying about and they soon go wrinkly and soft and lose their edge. Wash them in cold water, trim off the stems and keep them in a freezer bag in the fridge. They should last for at least a week.

49

Curry can improve your sex life – unofficial.

Many curry spices are widely believed to have an aphrodisiac effect on the body, notably cardamom, garlic, ginger and chilli. Green Thai curry is reckoned to have the highest turn-on factor as it includes the above, along with ginseng, lemongrass and basil.

50

Eat curry and stay healthy!

Scientists have identified huge health benefits from most of the spices in curries. The star is turmeric, whose active ingredient curcumin has been shown to combat many ills, from inflammation and high blood pressure to cancer and Alzheimer's. So keep eating the stuff!

Andrew Langley

Andrew Langley is a knowledgeable food and drink writer. Among his formative influences he lists a season picking grapes in Bordeaux, several years of raising sheep and chickens in Wiltshire and two decades drinking his grandmother's tea. He has written books on a number of Scottish and Irish whisky distilleries and is the editor of the highly regarded anthology of the writings of the legendary Victorian chef Alexis Soyer.

THE LITTLE BOOK OF
BARBECUE
TIPS
ANDREW LANGLEY

THE LITTLE BOOK OF
BEER
TIPS
ANDREW LANGLEY

THE LITTLE BOOK OF
HERB
TIPS
WILLIAM FORTT

THE LITTLE BOOK OF
POKER
TIPS

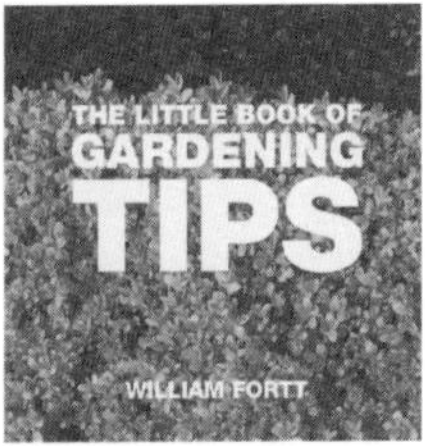
THE LITTLE BOOK OF
GARDENING
TIPS
WILLIAM FORTT

THE LITTLE BOOK OF
CHEFS'
TIPS
RICHARD

THE LITTLE BOOK OF
SPICE
TIPS
ANDREW LANGLEY

THE LITTLE BOOK OF
GOLF
TIPS
PETER FRENCH

THE LITTLE BOOK OF
TIPS
SERIES

THE LITTLE BOOK OF
CHEESE
TIPS
ANDREW LANGLEY

THE LITTLE BOOK OF
WINE
TIPS
ANDREW LANGLEY

THE LITTLE BOOK OF
AGA
TIPS²
RICHARD MAGGS

THE LITTLE BOOK OF
COFFEE
TIPS
ANDREW LANGLEY

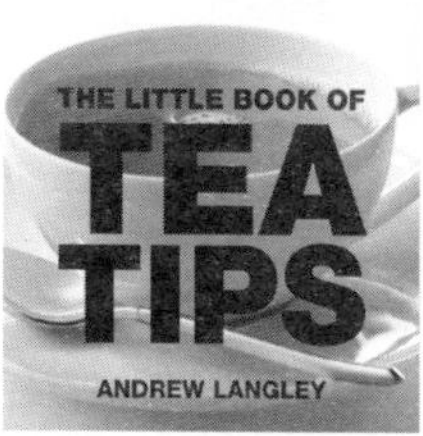
THE LITTLE BOOK OF
TEA
TIPS
ANDREW LANGLEY

THE LITTLE BOOK OF
AGA
TIPS³
RICHARD MAGGS

THE LITTLE BOOK OF
AGA
TIPS
RICHARD MAGGS

THE LITTLE BOOK OF
CHRISTMAS
AGA
TIPS
RICHARD MAGGS

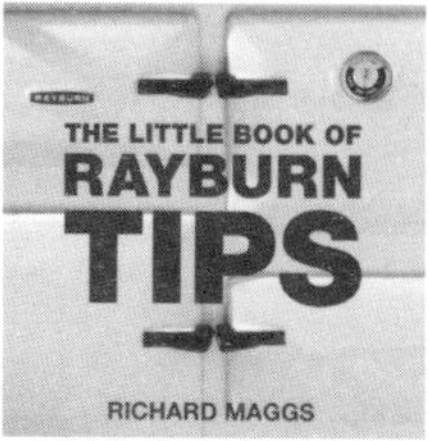
THE LITTLE BOOK OF
RAYBURN
TIPS
RICHARD MAGGS

THE LITTLE BOOK OF
BRIDGE
TIPS
PETER FRENCH

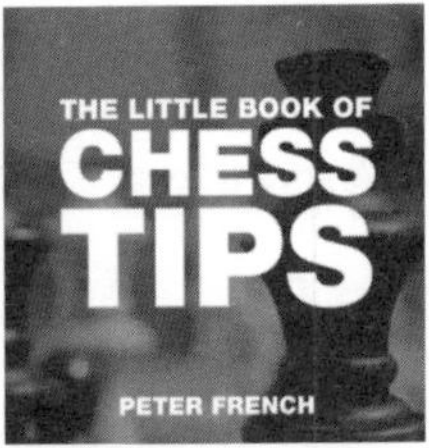
THE LITTLE BOOK OF
CHESS
TIPS
PETER FRENCH

THE LITTLE BOOK OF
FISHING
TIPS
MICK DEVENISH

THE LITTLE BOOK OF
GREEN
TIPS
WILLIAM FORTT

THE LITTLE BOOK OF
KITTEN
TIPS
ANDREW LANGLEY

MARMITE
PAUL HARTLEY
THE LITTLE BOOK OF
MARMITE
TIPS

THE LITTLE BOOK OF
PUPPY
TIPS
ANDREW LANGLEY

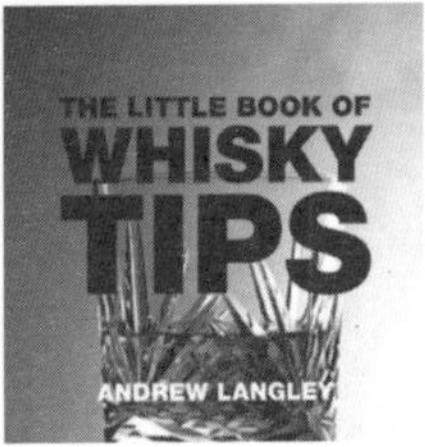
THE LITTLE BOOK OF
WHISKY
TIPS
ANDREW LANGLEY

THE LITTLE BOOK OF
TRAVEL
TIPS
MEGAN DEVENISH

Little Books of Tips from Absolute Press

Aga Tips
Aga Tips 2
Aga Tips 3
Christmas Aga Tips
Rayburn Tips
Tea Tips
Coffee Tips
Wine Tips
Whisky Tips
Beer Tips
Cocktail Tips
Cheese Tips
Bread Tips
Herb Tips
Spice Tips
Curry Tips
Marmite Tips
Olive Oil Tips
Vinegar Tips
Pasta Tips
Cupcake Tips
Cake Decorating Tips
Macaroon Tips
Chocolate Tips
Ice Cream Tips
Chefs' Tips
Barbecue Tips
Gardening Tips
Houseplant Tips
Golf Tips
Travel Tips
Fishing Tips
Green Tips
Frugal Tips
Poker Tips
Bridge Tips
Chess Tips
Backgammon Tips
Scrabble Tips
Puppy Tips
Kitten Tips